LIFE'S
Poems
LITERACY
for
LESSONS
Teachers

STEVEN L. LAYNE

INTERNATIONAL
Reading Association
800 BARKSDALE ROAD, PO BOX 8139
NEWARK, DE 19714-8139, USA
www.reading.org

The International Reading Association attempts, through its publications, to provide a forum for a wide spectrum of opinions on reading. This policy permits divergent viewpoints without implying the endorsement of the Association.

Director of Publications   Joan M. Irwin
Editorial Director, Books and Special Projects   Matthew W. Baker
Senior Editor, Books and Special Projects   Tori Mello Bachman
Permissions Editor   Janet S. Parrack
Production Editor   Shannon Benner
Editorial Assistant   Tyanna L. Collins
Publications Manager   Beth Doughty
Production Department Manager   Iona Sauscermen
Supervisor, Electronic Publishing   Anette Schütz-Ruff
Senior Electronic Publishing Specialist   Cheryl J. Strum
Electronic Publishing Specialist   Lynn Harrison
Proofreader   Charlene M. Nichols

Project Editor   Tori Mello Bachman

Cover Design and Illustrations   Linda Steere

Library of Congress Cataloging-in-Publication Data
Layne, Steven L.
    Life's literacy lessons : poems for teachers / Steven L. Layne.
      p.   cm.
ISBN 0-87207-299-1
1. Literacy programs—Poetry.   2. Teaching—Poetry.   3. Teachers—Poetry.   I. Title.
    PS3612.A96 L55   2001
    811'.54—dc21
2001003531

Dedication

*These poems are dedicated to the many people who
have contributed to my own literacy growth.
You have left an indelible impression behind, and
you are with me always.*

THANK YOU:
Mr. and Mrs. Richard Layne, Mrs. Wini Padgitt, Miss Mary Lou Porter,
Mrs. Retta Richardson, Mrs. Karen Fiedler, Ms. Holly Hahn, Mrs. Deborah Winger,
Ms. Tamara Tudor, Mrs. Barbara Bushong, Mrs. Darla Howlett,
Mrs. Charlotte Warner, Mrs. Marjorie Schott, Mrs. Kristen Stombres,
Dr. Jeanette Hsieh, Dr. Carol Fuhler, Dr. Pamela J. Farris, Dr. Mary Ann Wham,
Dr. Susan Davis Lenski, Dr. Jerry L. Johns, Mrs. Sandy King, Mrs. Kathy Smith,
Dr. Marguerite Bloch, Mrs. Carol Preseren, Mrs. Kathy Dickson,
Mrs. Mary Ann Cook, Mrs. Kathleen Bruni, Ms. Marilyn Jancewicz,
Mrs. Valerie Cawley, and, of course, Mrs. Deborah Layne.

Contents

Preface
–xiii–

_____

About Beginning and Early Reading

Reading Orphans
–3–

First Grade
–5–

For the Phonics Advocate
–6–

For the Whole Language Advocate
–7–

For the Balanced Instruction Advocate
–8–

A Poem Written Exclusively . . .
–9–

Aliteracy Poem
–10–

A *Word* About *Vocabulary* Instruction
–11–

Early Literacy Assessment
–12–

———————

About Grammar, Spelling, Handwriting, and Composition

The Ivory Tower
–17–

Grrrrr! for Grammar
–19–

Spellingitis
–21–

Milford's Mom
–23–

Mrs. Peacock: Craftsman at Work
–24–

Cursive Writing Sparks a Revolution
–26–

Mail Drop
–27–

Staff Development
–28–

Why the Teachers' Lounge Has a Door
–30–

A Poem About Kids Who Move . . .
–32–

Oops!
–33–

About Junior High and High School Literacy Issues

The Transfer
–37–

Why I Love Teaching Junior High
–39–

Stage Fright
–40–

Literature Circles
–41–

Dissection
–43–

Censorship
–44–

So Honored
–46–

Lifesaver
–48–

A Cautionary Poem for Content Area Specialists
–49–

About Reading Aloud

What Is It That You Like to Do . . .
–53–

Readin' Worries
–54–

Another Time, Another Place
–56–

Observations From on High
–58–

There's Something
–60–

Read to Them
–62–

———————

About Standards and Teachers

The Standards
–67–

Out-of-Date
–68–

Model Teacher
–69–

Sometimes Teachers Wonder . . .
–70–

. . . and Sometimes We Don't
–71–

Preface

*I*n 1994, I saw my first literacy poem in print in *The Reading Teacher.* "Read to Them" became a catalyst for many of my future writing and speaking endeavors. Over the next two years, I was bombarded with requests from all across the United States to use the poem for a variety of purposes. These requests reinforced to me that literacy educators have a great love for poetry.

Discovering the truth of personal experience inside a simple poem engenders a wonderful bond of community. We laugh or cry as we see our own experiences or those of our colleagues reflected in the words of a poem. No other written medium reveals the truth in quite so powerful or provocative a manner.

I love teachers, especially those with a heart for helping children learn to love reading and writing. This collection of poems was written to honor literacy educators for all that they do. It was written to reflect a truth that is sometimes humorous and other times very difficult to acknowledge. It was written to provoke thought and to inspire change.

For those of you who love "the scoop" on everything, I've included the *stories behind the poems.* For everything there is a beginning, and learning where ideas come from is an aid to writers of all ages. At the conclusion of each poem, I've shared a bit of the musings that led to the creation of that particular piece. Share these stories with your own students—only for those poems appropriate for a student audience, of course—to help them understand that the subject matter for a poem is all around them!

I hope there is something here for almost everyone. For those in higher education, I want these poems to serve as solid introductions to many of the topics you cover as you work to train the world's one best hope for change—our future teachers. For consultants, may these poems help launch topics that you bring into schools as you seek to fortify and aid teachers at all grade levels. Most importantly, for the literacy educators who give so tirelessly day after day to help young people in classrooms around the world—may these poems comfort and delight you, trouble and inspire you.

As I am out and about performing these pieces and new ones, I hope to meet many of you in person. Come up and say hello. Tell me about a literacy topic that you would like to read a poem about! Be good to the kids and to yourselves.

Your colleague in literacy,

Steve Layne

ABOUT

Beginning

AND

Early Reading

Reading Orphans

*R*eading orphans.
We're out there, you know.
Moved too many times, developmental delays,
Or maybe something just didn't click fast enough for the system.

It's amazing how we can be surrounded by other kids.
In a classroom year after year
And still feel alone, separate.

And the older we get, the greater the chasm.

We reading orphans look to you, our teachers,
Our one best hope for change.
You're frantic, frazzled, overworked, and underpaid,
We know.

But we look to you, still—

Using every attention-seeking behavior we possess
We're sending you a coded message . . .
Adopt Us.

 This poem was written on September 11, 2000, on a train
bound for Kirov, Russia. My wife and I were about to arrive
at an orphanage to pick up our wonderful son, Grayson, and
bring him home. Our journey made me think of the many
students with reading difficulties who so desperately need
their teachers' help.

First Grade

Squiggles.
Indecipherable, incomprehensible;
Foreign yet familiar.

Cherub faces eyeing pages
Filled to bursting with squiggles—
A banquet set for voracious appetites.

Prepare the meal with the utmost care,
Serve it on the fine china,
Don't forget the dessert.

Learning how to read shouldn't hurt.

 Sometimes we forget what text looks like to brand new eyes that are trying to make sense out of it!

For the Phonics Advocate

$\mathcal{T}$his week was spider week in first grade!
Our teacher read us a Big Book about spiders.
We looked at spider pictures.
We made spider hats and wore them every day.
We pretended to *be* spiders, and I chased Susie under a table!
We sang songs about spiders.
We finger painted spiders.
We told our teacher spider stories, and she wrote them down.
This week our spelling words were all about spiders!
Our teacher says this is the way we learn to read.
Learning to read is fun!
I'm going to read a book on my own now.
"W-E-B? Does anyone know what this word is?"

Next week is ladybug week in first grade.
I can hardly wait!

 I'll address the "Advocate poems" together because they really are a trio. The literacy "platforms" are really pretty funny when you think about it. If there were *one* best way, don't you think we would have found it by now?

6

For the Whole Language Advocate

$\mathcal{F}$irst grade is where we learn to read!

I learned what a digraph is on Monday, and I haven't been the same since.

On Tuesday, I found thirty-two consonant blends and won a Tootsie Roll in class!

Did you know that sometimes the letter *C* is hard and other times it is soft? Now that I have completed seventeen workbook pages, I'm sure to remember.

Thursday was a tough day. We played *Who Wants to be a* Reading *Millionaire*, and I made it to $250,000.00! A question about *schwa* threw me, and I lost it all.

When Friday afternoon came, the teacher let us vote on what we'd like to do: have an extra recess period or read?

Everyone enjoyed the kickball game.

For the Balanced Instruction Advocate

Scales, seesaws, and high-wire walkers—
A sense of balance makes them effective.

When you were told, "Throw out those basals, NOW!"
You heard, "You're narrow thinkers, and you've been doing it wrong all these years."

When you were told, "Write a scope and sequence for reading skills, NOW!"
You heard, "You've jumped onto a bandwagon, and you don't really know what you're doing."

Balance is a difficult state to achieve.
It takes dedication, perseverance, and equal support from all sides.

Teachers come equipped with those first two qualities.

Why doesn't everyone just stop bickering and help us out with that last part?

A Poem Written Exclusively for the Immense Pleasure of Those (Proud but Few) Who, 25 to 30 Years Ago, Had an SRA Kit in Their First-Grade Classrooms and Were Overachievers

*L*ife's crowning moment:
Arrival at *Aqua*.

 I loved first grade. My teacher, Mrs. Porter, has always been a favorite—she even came to my wedding! My fondest memory is of our SRA Reading Lab and of being the first one in the class to make it all the way to Aqua, which was the final color. I've since befriended several other "aquanites."

Aliteracy Poem

Mrs. Thompson's second graders are amazing!
The principal says they can comprehend anything—
Even a medical textbook.

Mrs. Thompson's second graders are incredible!
The superintendent says their oral reading is completely seamless—
Like the gentle flow of an eternal spring.

Mrs. Thompson's second graders are fantastic!
The P.T.A. president says they finished the reading workbook *and* the
phonics workbook before the end of the Third Quarter.

Mrs. Thompson's second graders worry me.
You see, I'm the aide who works in Mrs. Thompson's classroom,
And I know something that the others don't.

Mrs. Thompson's second graders don't like to read.

 The term *aliteracy* is still new to many people. I hope that this poem will help introduce the term to more educators. Aliterate individuals are those who can read but choose not to do so. I often ask my graduate students, "If we teach the children how to read, but none of them want to, have we done our jobs?"

A *Word* About *Vocabulary* Instruction

$\mathcal{T}$eacher says we gots to work on improving our

Volac~~b~~berry

Voba~~c~~larry

Vucb~~x~~caberry . . .

Words.

I recently read a very funny note from a parent who was trying to spell a word several different ways. She finally gave up and just wrote a simpler word.

Early Literacy Assessment

*Q*uiz them—both orally and on paper

Listen to their retellings

Have them read from the basic sight word list

Select a variety of papers that demonstrate their progress in spelling

Administer and score an attitude survey for each one

Give them the unit pretests and prepare the end-of-level posttests

Prepare a cloze passage for them

See if each one can segment a word into phonemes

Take a running record on all of them

Review their standardized test scores

Make audiotapes of everyone's oral reading for the portfolios

Check with the reading specialist on the progress of caseload kids

Now let's see . . . seems like there was something else I was supposed to do by the end of the week. Hmmmm. What *was* that?

Oh. Goodness me, I nearly forgot.

Teach.

Sometimes we get so busy preparing and administering assessments that we forget about the most important thing—teaching! This can also be true of those people removed from the classroom who are concerned with "monitoring student performance."

Grammar,
Spelling,
Handwriting,

Composition

The Ivory Tower

Sometimes I get awfully tired
Of listening to *the word* coming down from the Ivory Tower.
Then, I remember—they're only trying to help,
And I rush to the defense when my colleagues attack.

And yet, on days when the *latest* word defies belief,
I, too, am tempted to become a deserter.

Grammar *minilessons?*
The word—no more than ten minutes if you're doing it correctly.

A complete disaster in every classroom down our hallway.

But . . .

I have an idea.

There are exactly ten minutes
Between when music ends and physical education begins.
Could someone come down from the Ivory Tower
And teach plural possessives?

It seems that there would be just enough time.

Many teachers complain that university professors are too out of touch with the classroom. I defend the "higher ed" crowd when possible, but sometimes even I find the ideas being touted around the Ivory Tower a bit impractical.

Grrrrr! for Grammar

*G*rrrrr! for grammar
'Cause grammar is great!
Without it we'd face
An unthinkable fate.

Imagine, just try,
To conccive of a place
Where no one used grammar
Oh, what a disgrace!

Why how could we read?
And how *would* we write?
I'd say correspondence
Would be quite a fright!

With run-ons and fragments
In all of our print,
And no punctuation to help
Not a hint!

Our verbs and our subjects
Would never agree.
Antecedents for pronouns—
We never would see.

We'd be fraught by misspellings,
So make no mistake.
A land without grammar?
Just too hard to take!

My good friend and colleague, Valerie Cawley, is the
sharpest "grammarian" I've ever known. She has a
wonderful command of the English language; moreover,
she imparts to her students a desire to use language
correctly. Under her tutelage, they begin to care—truly
care—about the way in which they express themselves.
This poem was written for her, in appreciation for all that
she does to help kids.

Spellingitis

I think I have a bellyache
Because I need a spelling break
I'm sick of learning all these rules
Invented by some language fools

There's not a one that's made to last
No, none of them are hard and fast
But still they drill us night and day
Then slyly say, "Oh, by the way,

This only works when *that* is true
And such and such *can* be a clue
But *only* when a vowel may
Be used in a *specific* way

And even then, you've *really* got
To check *one other* caveat!"

Well, I can solve this language mess—
Let's cancel all the spelling tests!

The spelling rules of the English language are a constant
source of confusion. It's good to be reminded that not
everyone is a "speller" and to stay in touch with how the
younger crowd might feel about all of these rules and
exceptions.

Milford's Mom

*W*henever I call Milford's mom, the talking never ceases.
When Milford isn't doing well, she simply goes to pieces;
She wants him in at Harvard, and she wants him at the top,
You see, her endless prattling just never seems to stop.

On Monday she was crying, and on Tuesday she got sick,
'Cause Milford blew his "how to" speech and botched his magic trick.
On Wednesday she got loony, and on Thursday, boy, she screamed!
When Milford got a grade that she just *never* would have dreamed.

By Friday she had had it, and she started acting rude;
She heard my voice come o'er the phone, and WHAM! She came unglued.
She sobbed about his future, and she moaned about his strife—
Then she blamed each living being he'd encountered throughout life!

She exclaimed, "He'll never make it! I'm disturbed and so distressed!"
Then I said, "I only called to talk about his spelling test."

This poem mirrors the experiences many teachers have
when they make a phone call to talk about a minor issue
and get an earful of parental woes and concerns over
matters completely unrelated to the topic of the phone call.

Mrs. Peacock: Craftsman at Work

I have just created seventeen letter *p*'s
making absolutely certain that the *circle* part connects
with both the top line as well as that handy dotted center line
at precisely the points Mrs. Peacock suggested.

Prior to this amazing feat, I crafted,
with pinpoint precision, might I add,
fifteen heart-stopping letter *o*'s.

Each *o* was drawn to Mrs. Peacock's detailed specifications
including the small "curly-q" on top, which is not,
as Mrs. Peacock has pointed out on numerous occasions,
the hair on top of an empty smiley face.

Should my *p*'s pass inspection,
it has been suggested that tomorrow I shall graduate to *q*'s
which, Mrs. Peacock says, are the only truly elegant and pristine letters
in the entire English alphabet.

Who says second grade isn't chock full of pinnacle moments
and life-changing events?
Just ask Mrs. Peacock.

 Teachers at every grade level have yearly pet projects of
which they are immensely proud or certain skills or content
into which they pour their unbridled energies. Sometimes
it's good to see ourselves through the kids' eyes and have a
laugh at our own expense.

Cursive Writing Sparks a Revolution

*A*ttention everyone!

After spending the last thirty-three minutes
fussing over loops, curves, and slants,
I'd like us all to consider, once again, my earlier suggestion, made even
before all of this madness began.

Let's all agree to print for the rest of our lives and spend a lot more time
at recess!

Who's with me?!

 Why was cursive writing ever invented, and why do we want
children who can print decently to continue using cursive
when they can't write legibly in that form? I enjoyed using a
"kid" voice for this piece.

Mail Drop

$\mathcal{T}$eachers:

How would you like to receive over 100 letters
Every day
From people you didn't know
Who were only writing to you because
Someone told them that they had to?

Think about this
Carefully
The next time you start to assign your students
The task of writing

To
An
Author.

I promised myself, if I ever had the chance, I'd help all of
the authors who are begging teachers to stop *assigning* kids
to write letters to authors.

Staff Development

*T*he district's in chaos!
Writing scores are drooping like soggy diapers.

They hired a consultant this fall,
Auntie Mame of the writing world, we called her.
She reviewed the students' writing from last year and told us,
"The children should *never* write to a prompt.
These children are stilted, formulaic writers who lack tone, voice, and creativity.
That's the problem!

Just have them write about their *feelings*!
Let their unburdened, youthful ideas spill forth onto the pages
Like the rain showering down upon the parched Earth!"

The district then hired another consultant for the spring,
Writing Rambo, we called him.
After a review of the students' writing from the fall, he told us,
"The kids should *always* be writing to a prompt.
These kids are wispy, superficial writers who lack logical support, sufficient
elaboration, and proper conventions.
That's the problem!

Just have them write to practice prompts, preferably three per day!
Give them a clear, precise framework to latch onto.
Trust me, once they learn it, they'll *never* let it go!"

The district administrators are now pressuring us to spend our summer developing a new writing curriculum based upon the recommendations of the consultants whom they hired but never listened to.

They're paying us, of course.

We've decided to take the job and the money,
spend the summer vacationing with our families,
and turn in the original curriculum in new three-ring binders.

 I couldn't resist depicting an all-too-often-true scenario that occurs in many school districts. I've heard countless versions of this type of situation—except for the fictionalized ending, of course.

Why the Teachers' Lounge Has a Door

A seasoned teacher nervously bites her lower lip
The day of reckoning has arrived

The State Writing Test Administration Manual grins malevolently from
the top of the stack

Pencils sharpened, test booklets distributed, directions explained
Countless weeks of preparation are about to come to fruition

The principal enters and moves inconspicuously to the back of the room,
poised to observe

"Any last minute questions, boys and girls?"

A hand rockets skyward but forgoes acknowledgment,
"I thought you were going to *cancel* this writing test, Mrs. Catalano?"
The principal's cocked eyebrow collides with the teacher from across the room.
"Why, Cletus," she stammers. "That certainly is *not* the case! Whatever
gave you such a *silly* idea?"
A sly grin creeps onto the face of the precocious boy.

"I was walking by the teachers' lounge when you told Mrs. Gulliford that you were worried the state writing tests were going to turn us into a bunch of *mindless, mechanical* writing robots!"

Many teachers are concerned that the pressure we all feel to turn out students who can write well—specifically for the state tests—may lead to overdoing the preparation.

A Poem About Kids Who Move Into Your School District From a District Where They Do Too Much Training in Preparation for State Writing Examinations

"All right boys and girls,
Today, I'd like you to write a descriptive paragraph about something you treasure."

"Mrs. Smith, may I please write this in a five paragraph format using both internal and external transitions in combination with varying degrees of support and elaboration so as to enhance the precision and specificity of my response to the given writing prompt?"

"Matthew, dear, I just want you to write a simple descriptive paragraph."

"But Mrs. Smith, I moved here from West Hampton Hills.
That's the only way I know how to do it."

This poem reflects a true story that happened to one of my wonderful colleagues—Marilyn Jancewicz. We laughed for days over this one! Nobody can tell it quite like Marilyn, but here is my best effort.

Oops!

*W*hat do you *mean* those handouts you sent to my room five minutes before the bell rang and told me to stuff into the report card envelopes

(and that I randomly crammed into those envelopes in no systematized fashion)

were the students' *individual* reading and writing scores from the state assessment test?!

It's going to be a very long night.

"Hello, Mrs. McDetweiler, the *funniest* thing happened today! *Actually*, you'll probably find this quite amusing. You see . . ."

 True story. Unfortunately, it's mine!

ABOUT

Junior High

AND

High School Literacy Issues

The Transfer

Teaching in the junior high
—Oh what a thing to do!
To transfer up from second grade
They said, "What's wrong with you!

In junior high the kids don't care,
Just wait—some lazy lout,
Will tell you he won't read one book
Two months and you'll want out!"

"Those kids are *reading duds*," they say
"Their skills are just the pits,
And if they have to read in class—
You've never seen such fits!

In grade school's where you've got it made
Our kids still want to please,
And many of them love to read
And say that it's a breeze

But big kids *hate* to read and write
The testing shows they're low."
I face my colleagues and reply,
"That's *why* I want to go."

I've taught at the elementary level and at the junior high level, and I love them both for different reasons. Most educators I meet, however, prefer one over the other. My heroine is Dr. Jill Cole, who moves from first to eighth and second to seventh grade with incredible grace and professionalism. What's more—she's fabulous no matter where she is serving!

Why I Love Teaching Junior High

"

. . . and so kids,

denotation is really just a fancy synonym for definition;

whereas, *connotation* refers more to the positive or negative attributes

that we associate with a word.

For example, there are many words that we look up in the dictionary

that have a *neutral* denotation

but, in fact, when we hear them,

they evoke strong negative feelings in us.

Can anyone think of word that has a neutral denotation

but a very negative connotation?"

I smile, preparing to bask in the glow of success as one of my students

makes the connection. "Yes, Arthur. Do you have an example?"

"Oh, yeah, easy! *School!*"

 Some concepts are so difficult to teach, such as denotation versus connotation. Although this particular incident is fictionalized, it is the embodiment of my experience teaching junior high. When they *finally* get it, they get you, too!

Stage Fright

*K*nees knocking
Throat's dry
Speeches make me want to die!

Hands wringing
Voice shakes
Geez, oh boy, what *guts* it takes!

Eyes darting
Stomach churns
Three more weeks—then it's *my* turn!

 This poem was written in honor of my colleague, Kathy Bruni, who has trained students in the art of public speaking for many years. It's also written for all of those kids who are petrified to "stand and deliver" in front of a crowd. It's easy to forget just how far in advance their terror can truly begin.

Literature Circles

Circles of literature
Literature loops
Just pass out the books
And we'll get into groups

'Cause once my group's seated
We start to converse
And in no time we're quoting
Both chapter and verse

From a book we *enjoy*
And we *get it* no less!
We're in charge of our reading—
No need to get stressed

Let's keep the lit circles
And try them once more
These types of discussions
Are what reading's for!

 My students love the chance to talk about books. Having "jobs" to do is a drag, they tell me, but when we try it without the paperwork, they generally come back and ask for it. Perhaps they're a bit young to hold a book discussion with no framework at all. Still, when they want to try it, I always say, "Go for it."

Dissection

················

11:27 p.m.

I've just finished the seventh really terrific book that Mrs. Pennywise has assigned us for Academic English this year.

Too bad that, like all of the others, by the time her class ends at 10:04 tomorrow morning,

I'll hate it.

 In writing the poems for this collection, I kept my ears open. Sorry to say that sometimes, this is what I heard from high school students. Does every book have to be evaluated to the point that there's nothing left to enjoy?

Censorship

*P*arents are enraged—
"What are they doing to our children by exposing them to that book?
Don't they care?"

Teachers are defensive—
"They have no idea how this book is being used or for what purposes!
Don't they trust us?"

Administrators are frustrated—
"This is a no-win scenario that's blown way out of proportion.
How can we satisfy everyone?"

Students are exempt—
"Everyone's talking about us, but no one asks *us* if we've been *damaged*.
Won't anyone listen?"

Parents want to protect their children.
Teachers want to educate their students.
Administrators want to provide a safe learning environment.

And the kids . . .

They just want to enjoy a good read.

 Book censorship is a subject about which I am passionate. It is important to remember that, in most cases, would-be censors are acting out of a sincere desire to protect kids. Unfortunately, the media exploits the slightest hint of a question about a book to the point that entire communities are torn apart over issues that could be best handled outside the public forum.

So Honored

・・・・・・・・・・・・・・・・・

*W*hat do you *mean* my child can't be in honors?
Why everyone *knows* that if you aren't in *Honors* English
You spend the rest of your life flipping hamburgers!

What's wrong with you teachers?
Can't you see that he's gifted! Gifted! GIFTED!

Of course, you can't.
You can't see his giftedness because it's hidden behind . . . behind
His *learning disabilities*!

Yes, indeedy-do, he has learning disabilities.
You never discovered them! We hid them from you!
We know what *you* people do to children with learning disabilities.

No! None of that for *Terrence*. We hired Mrs. Farfanhoofer
for $200.00 a day to help little Terrence with all of his homework
for the last seven years. Ha! Ha! See, we fooled you. You never found out!

Now then, you'll *have* to put him in Honors English
Or else you'll be guilty of discrimination!
We'll complain to the principal, we'll call the superintendent,
We'll petition the Board of Education!
We'll *force* you to put him in Honors English!

Lucky for Terrence he has parents like *us.*
Parents who know what's best for him.

Placement in honors-level classes can be a migraine-creating ordeal for teachers. Sadly, this poem is based on a real-life conference.

Lifesaver

*E*very day, Mrs. Warner has them take out their journals and write

And, at one time or another, most of them unknowingly allow their fragile emotions to melt into words in a safe, private place.

In the frantic, stress-filled, high school day
Mrs. Warner hopes she's found a way

To save some kids' lives.

 I had a high school English teacher, Mrs. Warner, who really sparked my desire to write. We didn't keep journals per se, but I know a lot of teachers today are asking high school kids to keep them. Our teens are under such pressure; journal writing is a good way to let them release what's churning around inside. It seems like the kind of thing Mrs. Warner would do, too.

A Cautionary Poem for Content Area Specialists

"*I* teach science—not reading.
If the kids can't read by the time they get to me,
It's because you *elementary* teachers are asleep at the wheel!"

[Pause.]

"Hey . . . hey, wait a minute . . . now wait just a . . . AHHH!"

Poor man.
Simultaneously peppered by one hundred sixty-three sharpened pieces of anti-dust, high-velocity chalk.

He never had a chance.
God rest his soul.

 The opening of this poem is based on an incident that occurred in a school where I was doing some consulting work. By the end of the week, the middle school science teacher had "seen the light" (he really is a terrific guy), but I feared the elementary teachers were going to riot on that first day!

ABOUT

Reading Aloud

What Is It That You Like to Do ...

*W*hat is it that you like to do

With someone you care about

In a comfortable place

With a lot of expression

And with no interruptions?

READ ALOUD! (of course)

 This is just a fun "fooler" I've used to open several inservices on reading aloud to kids. I hide the answer at first. You wouldn't believe the answers people come up with! I thought it was so obvious what the answer should be.

Readin' Worries

I got some readin' worries and
They're buggin' me to beat the band
The stuff they're tellin' me in school
Is makin' me look like a fool!

Those digraphs are plumb hard to take
And *schwa* gives me a belly ache!
I'm sick to death of blends and such
And *no more vowels*—I've had too much!

The words I'm s'posed to know on sight
Are keepin' me up late at night!
And darn that word wall makes me frown
I'd like to say, "Let's tear it down!"

But teacher, she likes words a bunch
She reads to us right after lunch
And when she does I start to feel
That books just might have some appeal.

'Cause all us kids'll gather 'round
a-sittin', lyin' on the ground
As teacher reads aloud each day
My readin' worries melt away.

Every now and then, I like to write in my "backwoods" kid voice. I don't really know where it comes from—but I like it. My students like me to read to them in this voice. I use it for some other poems that aren't in this book and for the voice of Harris when I read aloud from Gary Paulsen's novel *Harris and Me*.

Another Time, Another Place

Another time, another place,
Another life to live;
A different past, a valiant journey,
A friend with magic charms to give.

A promise spoken to myself,
An earnest, solemn vow;
Before the children leave my care,
They'll understand. Some way. Somehow.

That pages worn and tattered bear a tale that's fond and dear,
To someone out there, somewhere, it's a tale we need to hear.
And so I spend my moments on a search that knows no end,
Looking for the perfect tale to tell a child who's searching for a friend.

Delight and wonder, terror, fear—both tragedy and care
When falling from the pages seem more possible to bear;
For sometimes, when I'm looking closely, hidden on a face,
I see a desperate need for me to take them
to another time, another place.

Reading remains the great escape. I think we have more
kids needing to escape today than we once did.

Observations From on High

....

*I'*d just begun Chapter 7 when Dr. Schleppenfeld,
Who has a bachelor's in education, a master's in English literature, a
doctorate in reading pedagogy, and a post-doctoral degree in literacy research,

and

who serves as our district reading coordinator,
popped into my room for a visit.

He saw my eighth graders sprawled all over the rug,
breathless with anticipation while I paused to acknowledge his entrance.

"Oh!" he said, glancing at the scene curiously;
He appeared quite perplexed.
He then stepped toward me, leaned in, and whispered into my ear,

"Don't worry. We'll just forget this ever happened, and I'll come back sometime when you're really teaching."

A scenario similar to this one was described to me by a good friend. It's hard enough to find junior high teachers who will make the tIme to read aloud to their kids, and then you have some bozo like this who . . . never mind.

There's Something

There's something in their eyes

There's something in their hearts

There's something in their souls

That longs to hear a story

There's something in their eyes,
That sparkles like a gem;
Each time I tell them of a book I'd like to read to them.

There's something in their hearts,
A yearning deep within;
They're hoping I will take them to a place they've never been.

There's something in their souls,
Which craves the chance to meet;
The characters who seem to somehow make their lives complete.

There's something in their eyes

There's something in their hearts

There's something in their souls

That longs to hear a story.

 It's very hard to explain to someone who has never read aloud to a roomful of children how very captivating and exhilarating the experience can be. I feel it is my greatest privilege as a teacher—at every grade level.

Read to Them
....

Read to them
Before the time is gone and stillness fills the room again
Read to them

What if it were meant to be that *you* were the one, the only one
Who could unlock the doors and share the magic with them?
What if others have been daunted by scheduling demands,
District objectives, or one hundred other obstacles?

Read to them
Be confident Charlotte has been able to teach them about friendship,
And Horton about self-worth;

Be sure the Skin Horse has been able to deliver his message.

Read to them
Let them meet Tigger, Homer Price, Aslan, and Corduroy;
Take them to Oz, Prydain, and Camazotz;

Show them a Truffula Tree.

Read to them
Laugh with them at Soup and Rob,
And cry with them when the Queen of Terabithia is forever lost;

Allow the Meeker Family to turn loyalty, injustice, and war
Into something much more than a vocabulary lesson.

What if you *are* the one, the only one, with the chance to do it?
What if this is the critical year for even one child?

Read to them
Before the time, before the chance, is gone.

 Of all the published writing that I have completed to date, this little poem has brought me the most attention. It is dear to my heart because it expresses so clearly my deep desire for people to understand the necessity of reading to children. There's so much the children miss out on if they are not read to throughout the grades!

ABOUT
Standards
AND
Teachers

The Standards

*H*ooray for the standards
They keep us all in line
They've shaped up our curriculum
The district looks so *fine*!

The "Sup." is really perky
And the principal is swell
Even Imogene LaBamba,
School Board Pres., is looking well!

The parents are rejoicing
That their kids can read and write
And the teachers—they're just smiling
'Til the next set comes in sight.

Standards help those invested in education to identify the
goals we are collectively working toward. They are also a
security blanket for people who aren't working in the
classroom. It's amusing that excellent instruction doesn't
necessarily change due to the release of standards; it just
gets typed under a new heading.

Out-of-Date

················

A standard is defined as something agreed upon by general consent
as a reliable basis for comparison.

The only problem that I have with *these* standards is
that all of the people who generally consented to them are dead.

 While standards are a "buzz" topic right now, they won't be
forever. When they aren't the hot topic, it's interesting to
see just how l-o-n-g they're allowed to stay in place without
ever being updated or reviewed!

Model Teacher

....

*W*hen he asks us to write,
Mr. Bensen writes, too
And if we read to him,
He says, "I'll read to you."

When the podium's open,
He shares willingly
What a model of teaching,
He's turned out to be.

 I created this man. He's the teacher we're all striving to become. Some days we're closer than others.

Sometimes Teachers Wonder ...

$\mathcal{D}$ear Mrs. Tuttingsgood,

Thanks for the extra time you spent with me on my spelling every Tuesday and Wednesday after school this year. The tootering really helped a lot.

Tommy

 This poem is based on a letter that my wife recently received. It had us laughing for hours. I still laugh out loud every time I think of it. Fortunately, she was his *math* tutor.

... and Sometimes We Don't

*W*e read about beautiful, impressive farewells
      in movies,
            in books,
                  on television,
                       in the news.
When they say goodbye, there's always a happy ending.

And all is well.

But they can always tell what's going to happen.
      It's scripted.
           It's right in front of their noses.
               They don't have to worry.
                  It doesn't matter.
This matters.

You've taught me so much, so many incredible things.
You've taught me the way to make my ideas fly
      My creations perfect
          My emotions detailed
            My thoughts soar
               And that deserves a thank you.

But how do you thank the person who changes your life?

I wish I knew.

But another thing that you taught me was to try. So here it goes.

Thank you Dr. Layne. Thank you so very much. Thank you for the way you've touched my soul, the way you've brought my writing to life. Thank you for the lessons you've taught me, the criticism you've given me, the memories you've created for me. Thank you for the opportunities you've offered me, the goals you've helped me achieve, the barriers you've helped me break, and the treasures you've helped me find.

And now advice.

Never stop. Never give up. Never hold back. And most importantly, never change.

You've found what every teacher strives for: the perfect way to teach.

Thank you for changing me.

You did.

(Written by Lauren E. Sprieser upon her graduation from eighth grade at Butler Jr. High School, Oak Brook, Illinois.)

This is the only poem in the collection that was not penned by me; rather, it was penned for me. My decision to include it was not based on a desire for self-gratification. I believe this poem is representative of a favorite note, card, letter, or perhaps poem that *you* have received . . . or one that is still to come! Such treasures remind us why we do what we do. I also wanted to give Lauren the exposure because I believe she will someday be a famous writer.

Award-winning educator Steven L. Layne has been teaching reading and language arts at both the elementary and junior high levels for over a decade. He also teaches undergraduate and graduate courses in reading education, language arts, and children's literature.

An acclaimed writer and speaker, Steve appears at numerous conferences and provides workshops throughout the United States and Canada. He has published two picture books and a young adult novel, as well as journal articles, textbook chapters, dramatic pieces, prose, and poetry.

Steve's many awards include the Illinois Reading Council's 1999 Junior High Reading Teacher of the Year Award, the 2000 ICARE for Reading Award, and two awards for his doctoral dissertation research. Most recently, Steve has been honored by the National Council of Teachers of English with the 2001 Edwin A. Hoey Award, given each year to one outstanding middle-level U.S. educator.

Steve resides in St. Charles, Illinois, with his wife, Debbie, and his son, Grayson. He can be contacted at drread@northstarbks.com.